Kate Lamont
Family, Food and Friends

*For Nancy,
Sincerely,
Kate Lamont*

For my grandmother
Angela

Kate Lamont
Family, Food and Friends

FREMANTLE ARTS CENTRE PRESS

Acknowledgements

The recipe for quick rough puff pastry on page 24 was inspired by Joanne Weir's *From Tapas to Meze*, Crown Publishing Group, 1994.

The recipe for tandoori paste on page 64 was inspired by Victoria Alexander and Genevieve Harris' *The Bather's Pavilion Cookbook*, Ten Speed Press, 1995.

The recipe for lemon polenta cake on page 91 is based on Ruth Rogers and Rose Gray's in *The River Cafe Cook Book*, Ebury Press, 1995.

Contents

Introduction	•	*nine*
Wine and Food	•	*eleven*
Pantry	•	*twelve*
Basics	•	*eighteen*
Stocks	•	*twenty-six*
Quick meals	•	*thirty*
Picnic	•	*thirty-eight*
Barbeque	•	*forty-eight*
Casual dinner	•	*sixty*
Dinner party	•	*sixty-eight*
Customer favourites	•	*seventy-six*
Personal favourites	•	*eighty-four*
Kate Lamont	•	*ninety-three*
Index	•	*ninety-five*

Introduction

I was blessed with a childhood where wine and food and the Swan Valley were such an integral part of the way my family lived that I didn't realise how special they were — I took those things for granted.

My sister Fiona and I learned how delicious fresh food is, and how marvellous it is to enjoy wine and food together. We also learned to have regard for agriculture, to have pride in production, to be entrepreneurial in a realistic sense and to believe that we could achieve anything with hard work and faith in our own abilities.

Only years later did the daily experiences that formed my personal ethos and provided the enthusiasm for my working life crystallise for me. When my sister and I started our restaurant we cooked what we had always loved to eat, and served wines that we had always enjoyed. We still do.

This book is a small collection of recipes that encapsulate, for me, simple food. Underlying each recipe is the understanding that fresh is best, and so is simple. To cook simply, regard for ingredients is everything. A meal of fresh asparagus and grilled fish can only be great if the ingredients are. Enhanced with some fruity olive oil, salt and pepper, and a glass of wine you have a beautiful meal.

I am an ingredient-driven cook rather than a recipe-driven one. Our restaurant and shop menus are determined by the best produce on the day. We have a repertoire of cooking techniques and styles and we make these skills fit the produce, rather than starting with a recipe and shopping for the ingredients. It is a great way to cook because it means everything you serve is fresh.

Kate Lamont, January 2000

WINE AND FOOD

There is so much written about wine and food matching that I'm hesitant to add more words to the debate. Wine was always on the dinner table at home which made it something integral, never separate, in a meal — it is unthinkable for me to eat dinner without a glass of wine!
I always look for balance, a comfortable companion, a situation where neither dominates when I choose wine to accompany my meal, or indeed when I am preparing food to go with predetermined wines.

PANTRY

There are some important pantry staples, and although they can be a bit of an investment initially, they'll help you cook delicious food. You don't need to purchase them all at once, and in many instances they'll only need replacing after several months.

Some of my pantry staples include:

A couple of types of olive oil — a fruity one for salads and cold sauces, and a more robust, peppery one for cooking and drizzling over grilled fish, wilted spinach and ripe tomatoes.

Red wine vinegar — to use when you need a savoury acid (as opposed to lemon juice) but don't want the flavour or sweetness of balsamic, such as in salsa verde and caesar salad dressing.

Balsamic vinegar — for use as a regular dressing on salads, especially tomatoes; you can also add a dash to winter casseroles to enhance flavour, and drizzle over grilled vegetables.

Fish sauce — crucial for Thai-flavoured food and dressings.

Lemon oil — really useful, especially when you don't have real lemons; with its zesty quality it's terrific to use in dressings, cakes and on chicken.

Anchovies — help build a saltiness and flavour in sauces and dressings, and are beautiful on grilled tomatoes and in mashed potato; buy good quality ones that aren't too bony.

Capers — can dress up salads, especially those with seafood, and are flavour builders in sauces, mayonnaises and dressings; small capers packed in salt have the best flavour.

Sea salt — has a clarity of taste that for me brings out the fresh flavours in food.

Olive oil

Which one should I use?

It would have to be one of the most commonly asked questions of me. The answer isn't a simple one. There are plenty of olive oils on the market — Italian, Spanish, Australian, some extra virgin, some cold pressed, some with 'vintages' on them. I suggest you keep trying different brands until you find the ones you like, and keep in mind that different oils are for different purposes.

I find it useful to think of olive oil in a similar way to wine. Factors that influence the taste and quality of olive oils include variety of olive, the climate and weather conditions in any particular year, and the method of processing. The oil you use will affect the taste of what you cook and serve, so you need to give some thought to the flavours you are looking for.

I suggest having a couple of different styles in your pantry. A fruity, green style for salsa verde and other dressings, such as Joseph from South Australia, and a more peppery one to marinate fish and prawns, and drizzle over ripe tomatoes or pasta, such as Colonna from Molise in Italy.

Olive oil can oxidise if stored incorrectly. If you purchase a large tin, decant into a smaller bottle and cork rather than leaving a big air space in the tin, and store your oil in a cool dark cupboard.

Seasoning

For me salt and pepper are valuable allies in the kitchen. They are flavour enhancers in a most basic form, and often under utilised. In almost every instance salt and/or pepper will give food life in terms of aroma and flavour. I advocate seasoning throughout the cooking process to get better integrated flavours, but in a cautious way. I always make a final addition at the end. If you are uncertain whether to adjust seasoning, take a little of the food, season that portion and decide about the rest of it.

Sea salt is popular with chefs because it has a very pure salty taste, unlike refined salt which has additives to help keep it from clogging up. Sprinkle flakes on tomatoes and salad greens, and fold through risotto and mashed potatoes. English Maldon salt and the French Fleur de Sel are great salts to look out for.

I prefer to use cracked black or freshly ground pepper from a grinder. The aroma has much greater pungency, and the flavour is fresher and more powerful.

Szechuan pepper, often called for in Asian dishes, is a type of pod from the prickly ash. It has a more scented aroma than conventional peppercorns and is marvellous mixed with sea salt and pepper served over fried squid and fish.

Pasta

I always think about the type of sauce I'm serving before I choose the type of pasta. My favourite sort of pasta is freshly made, as to me it has a velvety texture not found in dried pasta. I'm the first to reach for a packet of dried at home, however, when time is tight or effort lacking.

Generally, long thin pasta like spaghetti and linguine need thick smooth sauces that stick to them, like goats cheese or tomato types. Sauces that have small chunks of seafood, like a marinara sauce, should be served with shell shapes so that the pieces can be trapped in the hollows. Penne and fusilli shapes that have ridges and grooves can be served with pesto and meat sauces that sit in the ridges.

When buying dried pasta look for brands where the pasta shapes have a dull, almost rough finish. This means that the sauce is more likely to stick to the pasta than slip off and be left on the plate.

BASICS

These are recipes that we use every day. Stand-alone dishes they are not, but they'll enhance a fillet of fish, turn a packet of pasta into dinner, jazz up a plain risotto and turn a piece of bread into a decent snack. In the main these basics keep well, so they can be made on the weekend or when you have some spare time — you'll be grateful later in the week, when you feel less inspired and haven't been shopping.

Caramelised onions

makes 3 cups

Fabulous mixed into pasta, served with barbequed meats, tossed with snap peas and served with poached chicken, rolled up in slices of smoked salmon, or piled into warm omelettes. Cook them covered for about three-quarters of the cooking time as the honey may burn, then uncover and finish cooking until golden brown.

10 medium-sized onions
4 tablespoons honey
$1/2$ cup olive oil
2 tablespoons balsamic vinegar
salt and pepper

Peel onions and slice thinly. Put into a baking tray and drizzle with honey and olive oil. Cover with foil and bake in a moderate oven for 45 minutes. Remove foil, stir and cook for a further 15 minutes or until dark and caramelised. Season and stir in balsamic vinegar.

Will keep in the fridge for 2 weeks.

Roasted tomatoes
makes 24 halves

These will become a staple in your kitchen once you've tried them — they actually taste like tomatoes! Serve them folded into risotto, on grilled fish, with roasted garlic on toast, with scrambled eggs, make a sauce with them for grilled veal, or toss them with flatleaf parsley and serve with grilled prawns.

12 tomatoes
3 stalks parsley
1 bunch chives
1 bunch thyme
1 bunch oregano
salt and pepper
olive oil

Lay half the herbs on a steel tray. Core tomatoes and cut in half. Place cut side up over the herbs. Sprinkle with salt and pepper and drizzle with olive oil. Cover with rest of herbs and roast in moderate oven for 40–60 minutes until about half original size.

Keeps well for 4–5 days in the fridge.

Preserved lemons
to fill a jar of 2-litre capacity

These have a distinct flavour, which is more gentle than fresh lemons. Slithers of preserved lemon enhance couscous, are great threaded into salmon steaks, finely diced they can be mixed into fish patties, and they can also be added to dressing for chicken salad.

12 medium-sized lemons
200 g salt
2 cinnamon quills
10 coriander seeds
200 mls extra lemon juice

Cut lemons into four leaving them attached at the base. Pour salt into each lemon and reform the shape. Place lemons in a jar, packing them down tightly. Layer with spices as you go. Add extra lemon juice and seal the jar. Store in a cool, dark place for 2 to 3 months before using. Rinse before use, discarding the flesh and using the skins.

Will keep for up to a year, so do as many as you can when your trees are full of fruit.

Salsa verde

makes 2 cups

A delicious sauce for summer dining. Salsa verde is so fresh and vibrant, its pungency uplifts the most simply cooked meals. Drizzle over warm potatoes, poached salmon, grilled chicken and barbequed cray tails. I feel parsley is a staple, but the other herbs in the sauce can be varied.

2 cloves garlic
3 anchovy fillets
1 tablespoon capers, rinsed of salt
1 teaspoon pepper
$\frac{1}{3}$ cup fresh thyme leaves
$\frac{1}{3}$ cup fresh rosemary leaves
1 cup flatleaf parsley
1 bunch chives
80 mls red wine vinegar
400 mls olive oil

Process ingredients together in a food processor or, for a smooth sauce, blitz in a blender.

Best when used within a couple of hours, but will keep in the fridge for a couple of days.

Quick rough puff pastry

Inspired by Joanne Weir's From Tapas to Meze

This pastry is delicious, easy — especially after you have made it once — and so much better than any commercial brand you can buy. Take the time out to make it, it's worth it! Remember to work with cold ingredients and don't try making this on a forty-degree day. Use the pastry to make tartlets and pies, with either sweet or savoury fillings, or split and fill with cream and fruit.

$1\frac{1}{3}$ cups flour
pinch of salt
180 g butter
2 teaspoons lemon juice
$\frac{1}{4}$ cup iced water

Chill the flour and butter before using. Chop butter into the flour until it is the size of a thumbnail. Add water and lemon juice and mix gently. As best you can, press together into a rectangular shape, there will be chunks of butter showing. Sprinkle extra flour onto the workbench and roll the pastry into a long rectangle, 1 cm thick. Don't worry if the edges are a little ragged. Fold the ends in to meet in the centre and then fold together. This will make four layers. This is your 'first turn'. Turn the piece of dough away from you a quarter of a turn and roll again to form a long rectangle, 1 cm thick. Repeat the folding process. This is your 'second turn'. Turn the piece of dough away from you a quarter of a turn and roll again to form another long rectangle. This time fold the pastry in thirds as you would a letter. Cover and chill for an hour.

The pastry will keep for a couple of days in the fridge or in the freezer for a month.

STOCKS

There is no doubt that good stock makes food taste better. Stock can transform vegetables into a hearty soup, rice into risotto, and a plain sauce into a marvel.

Chicken and fish stocks are relatively easy to make, freeze well, and the ingredients are readily purchased at fresh food markets. Simple rules to remember are: wash any blood from the carcasses; only use cold water, never hot when making stock (hot water may dissolve any fat in the pan which will result in a cloudy and possibly greasy stock); skim the top of the stock as it cooks (a white scum may surface as the stock heats, this is protein and other impurities from the carcasses and it can also cloud the final stock); and use the freshest and best vegetables you can.

To obtain a more flavoursome stock sauté the vegetables for fish stock and roast the carcasses and vegetables for chicken stock. A great, flavoursome stock will set like jelly when cold.

Stock freezes well and is a most welcome (and often lifesaving) basic for any cook. It keeps in the fridge for 2–3 days, or frozen for up to a month.

Fish stock

2 fish heads
2 fish carcasses
2 carrots
1 celery stick
1 onion, cut in half horizontally
(remove roots, but leave skin)
1 bulb of garlic
6 peppercorns
slice lemon rind
6 parsley stalks
50 mls olive oil
250 mls white wine

Remove the eyes and gills from the heads. In a large stockpot sauté vegetables in olive oil for 10 minutes over low heat. Add fish, parsley stalks, peppercorns and lemon rind and turn heat to high. Add white wine and reduce for a couple of minutes. Cover with cold water and bring to the boil. Skim regularly. At boiling point, turn heat down and simmer gently for 30 minutes. Strain, discard vegetables and fish. Cool.

Chicken stock

3 chicken carcasses
2 carrots
1 celery stick
1 onion
1 bulb of garlic
6 peppercorns
10 parsley stalks
6 thyme stalks
1 cup white wine
50 mls olive oil

Roast carcasses and vegetables with olive oil until browned. Tip into stockpot, place baking tray on top of stove and add wine over medium heat. Scrape any meat and vegetables from the tray and add this to stockpot with herbs and peppercorns. Cover with cold water and bring to boil. Skim regularly. At boiling point turn heat down and simmer for 2 to 3 hours. Strain, discard vegetables and carcasses. Cool.

QUICK MEALS

*To me a quick meal has to be made in 20 minutes including prep time and cooking time. It can't be complicated to make because there is every chance I'm really tired, talking to someone, or trying to watch the news on TV.
I also know that you need to be able to buy the ingredients from an after-hours market and that the meals have to be satisfying and tasty.*

Linguine with goats cheese, spinach and corn

serves 6 as an entree, 4 as a main course

I use goats cheese in lots of pasta dishes because it has a terrific texture as a sauce. While it does melt, it holds some form which means you have a sauce with substance rather than a 'creamy' sauce. The mild flavour of fresh goats cheese combines well with spinach (I often make a salad with crumbled goats cheese, spinach and slices of roasted field mushrooms), and corn cut straight from the cob gives crunch and body to the sauce. You could use roasted pumpkin pieces instead of corn, and fold in finely chopped basil leaves as you serve.

500 g linguine or spaghetti, fresh or dried
4 cobs of fresh corn
1 bunch English spinach
3 fresh goats cheese, about 150 g each
1 bunch chives
4 tablespoons toasted pinenuts
100 mls olive oil

Remove kernels from corn by slicing down the cob. Wash spinach. Snip chives into $2^{1}/_{2}$ cm lengths. Break goats cheese up into small pieces about the size of a large grape. Cook pasta and drain, toss in a little oil and keep hot. In a flat pan warm olive oil, add corn and cook for a couple of minutes until it starts to brown. Add goats cheese and warm until cheese starts to run (about 2 minutes). Add spinach, pinenuts and chives. Mix with pasta. Season with salt and pepper. Serve.

Grilled chicken, spinach salad, mustard dressing

serves 6

This chicken salad should probably be in my personal favourites section, because it's quick to make, wholesome and good for you, yet so delicious!
I always use thigh as it is moister and has more flavour than breast. I love spinach as a salad, and for this meal ensure that you buy young, small unblemished leaves. Roasted tomatoes are about the only addition I would make to this salad. The dressing seems like a major ingredient itself. If you aren't a fan of seeded mustard substitute a mild Dijon and use a great quality, fruity olive oil.

12 small chicken thighs, boned and skinned
200 mls olive oil
salt and pepper
2 bunches English spinach
1 avocado
2 tablespoons seeded mustard
50 mls sherry vinegar

Trim thighs if needed, season and marinate in 50 mls olive oil. Grill or barbeque until crispy. Wash and dry spinach. Slice avocado. Make dressing with mustard, vinegar and remaining oil, season. Dress spinach with half the dressing and divide evenly onto four plates. Slice thighs in half and place on spinach with avocado. Drizzle remaining dressing over chicken. Serve.

Mushroom soup with crispy bacon pieces

serves 6

Mushroom soup has an intrinsic richness for me — I'm not sure if it's from childhood memories of the real field mushroom (as opposed to the same shaped but different tasting ones we now see as 'field' mushrooms in store all year round rather than after the first winter rains). Regardless, it's one soup that is quick and easy to make and can be a meal in a bowl.

750 g button mushrooms
4 large field mushrooms
2 onions, diced
2 cloves garlic, minced
2 medium potatoes, peeled and diced
100 mls olive oil
2 litres chicken stock
⅓ cup fresh thyme
salt and pepper
200 g bacon, finely sliced
⅓ cup flatleaf parsley, chopped roughly

Wipe any dirt from mushrooms. Sauté onions and garlic over medium heat with potatoes until onion is translucent. Season. Slice mushrooms roughly and add to onions. Lower heat and cook covered for 15 minutes. Add stock and simmer for 20 minutes. Blitz in food processor with fresh thyme. Season with salt and pepper. Fry bacon until crisp. Drain away any excess fat and mix bacon with parsley. Serve soup hot, topped with bacon and parsley mixture.

Rhubarb and raspberry roly-poly

serves 6

Sophie, a marvellous cook who worked with us in the Swan Valley and in the city, made rhubarb roly-poly one day as a dessert special. It seems like it has never come off the menu in winter since then. It is quick to make and has a genuine comfort food feel to it. You can use apple, pear, strawberries — instead of rhubarb and raspberries — in combination or alone. You can also use orange juice instead of water in the syrup.

Syrup

500 mls water
1 cup sugar

Dough

2¾ cups plain flour
4½ teaspoons baking powder
½ teaspoon salt
180 g butter
250 mls milk

Filling

2 cups rhubarb cut into 1 cm pieces
1 cup raspberries (fresh or frozen)
⅓ cup caster sugar
½ teaspoon ground cinnamon
50 g butter

Sift dry ingredients together. Using your fingers rub the butter into the flour. Add milk and mix to a soft dough. Roll into a large rectangle. Scatter filling ingredients over the entire area of the dough. Roll into a loose cylinder and cut into 2 cm slices. Place in a baking tray, leaving room for expansion. Meanwhile, make the syrup by dissolving sugar in water and bringing to boil. Pour hot syrup over the slices in the baking tray. Bake in moderate oven for 35–40 minutes. Serve with cream.

PICNIC

As kids we used to go on picnics to Gidgegannup in winter. We usually took a barbeque, put the bottles of wine in the creek and laid old rugs over the least stony spot in the bush. We nearly always saw kangaroos and often, more so in spring, bobtail lizards basking in the sun. There was a game of cricket at some stage and always a casualty in the creek. I still remember all the little containers of different foods that had to be packed and unpacked and then packed up and unpacked at home, plus all the eating utensils and plates and barbeque plate. Looking back on it, maybe it was one of those experiences where mothers didn't really have a restful day!

These days my picnics involve preparing a platter of food and taking it down to the river, to an outdoor cinema, to the beach, to a concert or to the cricket — where I watch, not play! The only implements I take are linen napkins and wine glasses.

Most of these recipes can be made in advance the day or evening before. This food is meant to be eaten cool or at room temperature, and, of course, you don't need to be going on a picnic to make or enjoy eating it. All of this food makes great finger-food snack ideas and will hold in good condition when transported.

Quick puff pastry tarts

makes 18 bite-size tarts

1 batch rough puff pastry
(recipe on page 24)
3 eggs
250 mls cream
salt and pepper

Roll pastry into $\frac{1}{2}$ cm thick rectangle. Use a biscuit cutter to cut circles to fit muffin tins. Chill for 30 minutes. Whisk eggs with cream and season. Fill tarts with selected fillings and cover with egg mixture. Bake for 20 minutes in moderate/hot oven. Serve warm with salad greens or take cooled on picnic.

Suggested fillings (to make 18 tarts per filling)

1. 200 g crumbled blue cheese and 6 glacé figs cut into slithers
2. 250 g roasted pumpkin cubes and 100 g thinly sliced gruyère
3. 18 anchovies and 3 finely sliced roasted red capsicums
4. 250 g fresh salmon and $\frac{1}{2}$ cup finely chopped basil leaves

Chicken rissoles with lemon oil

makes 14 walnut-sized rissoles

500 g chicken mince
½ cup chopped parsley
salt and pepper
1 teaspoon lemon oil
6 slices day-old bread

Process bread to coarse crumbs. Combine all ingredients. Shape into balls and sit on a baking tray. Cook in a moderate oven for 15 minutes. These are also great barbequed.

Potato slice with tapenade

to fit a 26 cm x 26 cm x 5 cm tin

2 large potatoes
1 medium zucchini
1 onion
200 g cheddar cheese
1 cup self-raising flour
250 mls cream
6 eggs
2 tablespoons olive oil
1 tablespoon chopped dill
salt and pepper

Boil potatoes with their skin on for 10 minutes, peel skin off and dice into 1 cm squares. Grate zucchini. Finely dice onion and sauté in olive oil with potato squares on a medium heat until potato starts to crisp on the edges. Cool slightly then mix with all other ingredients and pour into a greased and lined tin. Bake in a preheated 180°C oven for 25 minutes. Cool. Cut into wedges and serve topped with tapenade.

Tapenade
makes 2 cups

2 cups pitted olives
(I like to use Kalamata)
4 anchovies
2 tablespoons lemon juice
1 tablespoon olive oil
pepper
2 tablespoons salted capers,
rinsed of salt

Process ingredients together. Serve on potato slice (recipe on page 43), as a dip on toasts and with barbeque steak.

Keeps well for up to 3 weeks in the fridge.

Spicy lamb with yoghurt in flatbread

250 g lamb mince
2 cloves garlic, minced
1 small onion, minced
1 teaspoon sweet paprika
1 teaspoon cumin
½ teaspoon harissa
1 tablespoon tomato paste
½ cup thick plain yoghurt
1 flatbread
2 Lebanese cucumbers

Fry spices with garlic and onion. Add lamb and brown. Season with salt and add tomato paste. Cook over medium heat for 15 minutes. Cool. Add yoghurt. Slice cucumbers thinly. Slice the flatbread in half lengthways, and then through the middle leaving a pocket. Spread with lamb mixture down the centre and fill with cucumber. Close to make a sandwich. Slice into bite-sized pieces.

Caramel slice

to fit a 32 cm x 26 cm x 5 cm tin

Pastry

180 g butter
130 g sugar
300 g flour
½ teaspoon baking powder
1 teaspoon vanilla essence

Cream butter and sugar with vanilla. Fold in dry ingredients. Reserve 50 g. Cook in moderate oven for about 20 minutes, or until golden brown and firm to touch.

Filling

250 g butter
800 g condensed milk
4 tablespoons golden syrup

Melt together over a bain-marie, or in a bowl suspended over a pot of simmering water. Stir to a smooth paste. Spread over cooked base.

Topping

125 g chocolate
125 g raw macadamia nuts
50 g reserved pastry,
broken into small pieces

Pulse or chop chocolate and nuts roughly. Sprinkle over the top of the filling with the reserved pastry. Bake in moderate oven for a further 20 minutes.

Cool in tin and cut into squares to serve. Store in an airtight container.

BARBEQUE

The anticipation of the first barbeque of the season seems to herald summer! For me a barbeque after my dad came home from cricket on Saturday nights was a constant during most of my childhood. In those days steak, lamb chops and sausages were the norm. Occasionally onions were put on as a way of 'cleaning the top and checking if it's too hot.'

Wow! How the barbeque has changed. Not only in its built form, but in the foods we cook and the levels of sophistication in the way we cook them. The romance of an open fire has been usurped by the convenience and consistency of gas, and the accessibility of fresh seafood has pretty much changed the face of the Aussie barbie. What has thrived is the concept of relaxed, simple, shared dining. With a clean cooking surface and a cook who doesn't want to char everything to a cinder, the world is your oyster.

Barbequed squid
serves 4 or more as part of a meal

Onion has to be one of the great flavours of summer, so they are a must for me at any barbeque. The smell of onions cooking is probably one of the most recognised aromas in backyards all over town. This recipe adds sliced fennel and onion to quick-cooked squid, and is delicious with a dollop of chilli mayonnaise. I also love to add, right at the last minute, rocket leaves or English spinach, which pick up the smoky flavours of the grill instantly.

2 fresh squid each weighing about 1 kg (uncleaned)
1 fennel bulb
2 onions
½ cup plus 2 tablespoons olive oil
1 tablespoon balsamic vinegar
salt and pepper

To clean the squid, hold the body in your left hand and the tentacles in your right, then pull apart firmly — like a Christmas cracker. Hook the transparent backbone out of the tube (in your left hand) with your finger. Wash the squid tube and peel off the pinkish skin if you wish. Wash tentacles and scrape any tough suckers from them. Slice squid into chunky bite-sized pieces and marinate in the oil, salt and pepper. Peel and trim onions and fennel and slice into 5 mm slices. Reserve some of the fennel fronds to scatter over the cooked squid. Barbeque onion and fennel mix in 2 tablespoons of olive oil, then push to a just-warm side of the barbeque plate. Cook squid over high heat for about 5 minutes. Do it in batches if you have a small grill plate as you need to avoid 'stewing' the squid. Combine squid with onion and fennel mix, splash with balsamic vinegar and toss in fennel fronds. Serve.

Chilli mayonnaise
makes 2 cups

Delicious with barbequed squid and other seafood.

2 egg yolks
200 mls vegetable oil
300 mls fruity olive oil
1 teaspoon chilli flakes
1 tablespoon fresh dill or fennel fronds
½ teaspoon salt
½ teaspoon pepper
50 mls lemon juice

You can make mayonnaise in a food processor or by hand, but either way you need to add the oil slowly so it can emulsify with the egg yolks to make a smooth sauce. Put egg yolks, salt and pepper and lemon juice in a food processor and, with the motor running, trickle the oil down the chute gradually until the mixture begins to thicken, or whisk the oil in by hand. You can add it a little faster once about half the oil is added. When all the oil is incorporated, fold in the chilli flakes and dill. Check for taste as you may wish to add more salt or lemon juice.

Keeps for one week, covered in the fridge.

Grilled quail

serves 8 as an entree or 4 as a main course

One of the most popular dishes in the restaurant over the years has been quail. We've always served them partially boned, usually cooked on a flat grill so their skin becomes crispy. A butcher will sell quail with the main carcasses boned out, which means no preparation — just marinate and cook.

8 quail, partially boned
1 teaspoon fennel seeds
1 teaspoon coriander seeds
1 teaspoon cumin seeds
1 teaspoon sea salt
100 mls vegetable oil

Dry roast spices or cook in a pan for 3–4 minutes, then grind together with salt. Marinate the quail in the spices and oil for up to two days. Grill or barbeque over relatively high heat for 10–15 minutes.

Lamb fillets with coriander sauce

serves 4 or more as part of a meal

Lamb fillets are tender, flavoursome and quick to cook. Be careful to trim them up and remove the silver 'skin' from their tops. This will allow them to cook straight and flat.
The coriander sauce is lively and fresh.

1 kg lamb fillets
3 cups coriander leaves
⅓ cup cumin seeds
1 teaspoon salt
1 teaspoon cinnamon
240 mls olive oil
90 mls white vinegar
1 teaspoon sugar

Roast cumin seeds until toasted and aromatic. Blitz with all other ingredients except lamb. Trim lamb fillets and marinate in a little olive oil, salt and pepper. Barbeque and serve warm with the coriander sauce.

Couscous with roasted pumpkin and cashews

serves 4 or more as part of a meal

The salads to go with this meal are quick to make, and you can vary the ingredients to suit your fridge contents and personal tastes. Couscous is simple to prepare and you can add slices of preserved lemon, plump raisins, caramelised onion, and fresh tomato slices instead of or in addition to the recipe ingredients.

500 g couscous
600 mls chicken stock
1 kg pumpkin
½ cup caramelised onions (recipe on page 20)
½ cup roasted cashews
1 cup chopped parsley
salt and pepper
50 mls balsamic vinegar
120 mls olive oil

Heat the stock to a simmer, pour over couscous and leave for 10 minutes. Stir to break the couscous up into individual grains. Season. Roast the pumpkin drizzled with olive oil and seasoned with salt and pepper in a moderate oven until just soft. Mix all ingredients together gently and serve.

Greens with blue cheese croutons and field mushroom slices

serves 8 as part of a meal

Crunchy croutons add texture to a lettuce salad, and spread with blue cheese also add umph to the dish. Try barbequing the mushrooms and adding them warm to the salad as you serve.

500 g mixed greens
4 field mushrooms
16 x 4 cm rounds of sourdough or other sturdy bread
150 g creamy blue cheese
small bunch fresh thyme
4 tablespoons plus 100 mls olive oil
30 mls balsamic vinegar
salt and pepper

Roast in a moderate oven or barbeque the field mushrooms with fresh thyme, salt and pepper and 4 tablespoons of olive oil. Slice. Spread the cheese on the rounds of bread and heat in moderate oven for 3 or 4 minutes, or grill until melted. Make a dressing with the vinegar, the remaining olive oil and salt and pepper. Toss the mushroom slices, the warm croutons and the dressing with the greens and serve.

Orange almond cake

makes one large cake to fit 23 cm tin

This cake recipe is not my own invention — there are many variations — and with good reason, it's a beautiful cake! When you make it be sure to squeeze most of the liquid from the oranges otherwise it tends to be more like a pudding than a cake. Serve with cream.

3 oranges
9 eggs
375 g caster sugar
375 g almond meal
2 teapoons baking powder

Simmer whole oranges for 2 hours, changing water 3 times. Cool. Halve. Remove seeds and squeeze out liquid. Puree eggs and sugar, add oranges. Fold in almond meal and baking powder. Bake at 180°C for 40–50 minutes. Dust with icing sugar to serve.

CASUAL DINNER

For me casual dining is dining! Platters of food brought to the table to be shared amongst family and friends with crusty bread and lots of wine.
As our business grew we spent more and more time sitting around the table as a family. The concept of platters rather than individual plates seemed to take over the way we ate our meals. Talking most often about work, the food would sit on the table for a few hours, and the salad and bread would stay on the table as we brought out cheese to go with that last bottle of red we couldn't resist opening. These habits now dominate my leisure time and I'm always looking for ideas that mean I can stay at the table for the whole time, since I don't want to miss a minute of conversation! Hence these recipes are easy, have no hard-and-fast methods or rules, are driven by fresh and perfect ingredients and made with minimum preparation time.

Asparagus with roasted garlic dressing

serves 6

Asparagus seems to be less and less of a seasonal vegetable. You can now purchase it virtually all year round. However I have always thought of it as a spring eating experience, just like strawberries. Look for even, quite gentle green-coloured stalks that have a sturdy appearance. Avoid stems that have woody-looking stalks or budding, loose tops. I always cook asparagus simply, steamed, grilled or blanched, and serve warm or cold, with a minimum of fuss. The roasted garlic dressing is divine, versatile and delicious on warm or room-temperature asparagus.

1 kg fresh asparagus spears
2 bulbs garlic
250 mls plus 1 tablespoon olive oil
100 mls red wine vinegar
1 tablespoon honey
salt and pepper

Place whole garlic bulbs on an oven tray, season with salt and pepper and drizzle with one tablespoon of olive oil. Roast in a moderate oven for 30 minutes. Cool. Squeeze the cooked garlic from the skins and whisk with the olive oil, honey and vinegar. Season. Trim the ends from the asparagus. Blanch in boiling salted water for 3 minutes. If serving cold, refresh in cold water. Otherwise serve immediately with a dollop of dressing.

Tandoori fish salad
serves 6

Serving room-temperature food is so appropriate for lazy afternoons around a lunch table. I also believe that many foods show more interesting and robust flavours if they are served warm or cool rather than hot or cold. The idea of pasta 'salad' is such a dish. Add fish straight from the oven to room-temperature pasta and other ingredients and serve.

500 g pasta
750 g pink snapper or similar
tandoori paste
18 roasted tomatoes
(recipe page 21)
1 bunch chives,
snipped into 2 cm pieces
1 cup ligurian (or nicoise) olives
2 tablespoons balsamic vinegar
1 tablespoon olive oil

Tandoori paste

8 peeled garlic cloves
5 cm piece of fresh ginger
2 medium tomatoes,
skinned and deseeded
2 teaspoons roasted ground
coriander seeds
1 teaspoon tumeric
1 tablespoon natural yoghurt
1 tablespoon chilli powder
½ teaspoon fennel powder
1 tablespoon vegetable oil

Blend all tandoori paste ingredients together. Spread tandoori paste over fish fillets. Bake in preheated oven at 180°C for about 15 minutes. Cook pasta, drain and refresh. Toss in olive oil to coat. When fish is still a little warm, mix together with all other ingredients. Serve at room temperature with salad greens and bread.

Cos lettuce salad
serves 6

A crisp salad should be served with this meal and baby cos lettuce leaves, whose boat shapes can hold delicious dressing, are perfect. This dressing is also great on steamed vegetables.

½ kg baby cos leaves or 2 medium cos lettuces, washed
3 tablespoons soy sauce
3 tablespoons sesame oil
3 tablespoons rice wine vinegar
125 mls olive oil
1 clove garlic, minced
1½ cm piece of ginger, minced

Make dressing with all ingredients, except lettuce. Just before serving toss salad leaves through dressing and serve.

Mascapone cream with strawberries

serves 6

We can't remember where this mascapone cream recipe came from but we remember how much we love it! It is also lovely with grilled peaches. The idea of making a little strawberry sauce to mix in with the rest of the berries turns fruit into dessert.

500 g mascapone
1 cup icing sugar, sifted
2 tablespoons Galliano
3 egg whites
4 punnets ripe strawberries
½ cup caster sugar

Whisk mascapone with half the sifted icing sugar until smooth. Whisk egg whites to soft peaks with the rest of the sugar. Fold the two mixtures together carefully until smooth and light. Stir in Galliano and chill. Wash and hull berries. Choose a dozen of the least perfect and process with sugar until smooth. Halve the rest or leave whole depending on the size. Mix with the sauce. Serve with a dollop of mascapone cream.

DINNER PARTY

My mother is a great cook and our family took enormous pleasure in the wine and food culture. In the mid seventies the restaurant and dining scene certainly wasn't what it is today, so my parents entertained regularly in their home. It also seemed that this was the start of the gadget era in domestic kitchens when food processors revolutionised what could be achieved.

As a child I can remember getting up early the morning after one of Mum's dinner parties to seek out leftovers: fresh sage stuffed roast pork, once-crispy potatoes and chocolate mousse.

For my generation though, time is of the essence and taking half a day to create a special dinner is not a priority, so cafe culture burgeoned, and we look to casual dining in our homes and outdoor living spaces.

Occasionally, though, taking time to prepare a special dinner, shopping for out-of-the-ordinary ingredients and setting the table with linen is something that I love to do. Even then I still stick strongly to my ethos of fresh and simple. I've never been an advocate of spending all night in the kitchen while my guests drink my favourite wines without me!

Grilled salmon with sweet Thai-style dressing

serves 8 as an entree

Fresh salmon is wonderful and quite special. It should be cooked gently and handled with care. The Thai-style dressing emphasises the clean and bright flavours of the fish.

8 x 150 g salmon steaks
mild-flavoured olive oil for cooking
salt and pepper
2 cups washed coriander leaves and stalks

Season and brush salmon with oil. Pan fry salmon over medium heat for about 5 minutes, turning once. Serve warm with dressing on a bed of coriander leaves.

Sweet Thai-style dressing

1 cup white vinegar
150 g caster sugar
zest from 2 limes
6 tablespoons lime juice
4 tablespoons fish sauce
1 red and 1 green chilli, seeds removed and sliced finely
1 cup coriander leaves and stalks, washed and finely chopped

Dissolve sugar in vinegar and boil rapidly for 2 minutes. Cool. Mix coriander with all other ingredients.

Veal steaks with porcini mushrooms

serves 8

Speak to your butcher about the veal. Locally we can purchase marvellous milk-fed veal which is beautifully tender, I suggest asking for steaks cut from the rump. At the restaurant we use the eye of the loin, but you could use a veal T-bone for this dish, which would ensure moist meat but isn't quite as elegant.
The porcini mushrooms have quite a rich flavour and can be mixed with regular mushrooms if you find them a little strong. Use chicken stock to reduce the mushrooms with any pan juices to give the best flavour.

8 veal steaks
40 g dried porcini mushrooms
4 cups chicken stock
½ cup white wine
1 teaspoon balsamic vinegar
salt and pepper
100 mls olive oil

Soak porcini in 1 cup of warm water for 30 minutes. Drain, reserving liquid. Slice mushrooms and put to one side. Reduce chicken stock to a volume of 1 cup by boiling rapidly. Season veal steaks with salt and pepper and drizzle with olive oil. Pan fry over high heat to seal the meat, lower heat to medium and cook to your liking. Remove veal from pan and keep in a warm place. Place pan back over a medium heat and add mushrooms. Sauté for a couple of minutes. Return heat to high. Add balsamic vinegar and white wine. Stir bottom of pan to loosen any caramelised meat juices. Reduce by half. Add reserved porcini water and reduce, again by half. Add chicken stock, and simmer until you have a syrupy sauce. Taste and season. Keep warm. Serve veal with roasted vegetables and sauce.

Roasted vegetables

I like to cut the vegetables small and usually cook them in batches since they take different cooking times.

3 medium carrots
wedge of Queensland Blue pumpkin
16 baby courgettes
2 red onions

Prepare vegetables by peeling carrot and pumpkin and cutting into slightly larger than bite-sized pieces. Place on baking tray, drizzled with olive oil and sprinkled with sea salt and pepper, and roast for 30 minutes. Prepare courgette and red onion in a similar way, and roast together for 20 minutes.

Meringues with passionfruit curd

My grandmother makes the best meringues, and because of this I love them! Any special dinner at my place means my guests have to endure meringues again. Served with thick cream and passionfruit curd I'd have to say they are my favourite dessert.

Meringues
makes 36

3 fresh egg whites
6 rounded tablespoons caster sugar

Beat egg whites in a large bowl until stiff. Gradually add sugar, beating continuously until mixture stands in firm peaks. Spoon rounded dessertspoon-sized shapes onto a greased or Gladbake-lined tray. Bake in preheated oven at 100°C for $1^{1}/_{2}$ hours. Turn oven off and leave meringues in for a further hour. When cooled, store in an airtight container. Meringues keep well for up to 2 weeks.

Passionfruit curd
makes 500 mls

230 g unsalted butter
460 g caster sugar
180 mls passionfruit pulp
5 eggs, beaten

Melt butter and sugar together in top of a double saucepan. This will take about 15 minutes. Whisk in eggs and passionfruit, stirring constantly. Cook over medium heat until mixture coats back of spoon, about 15 minutes, stirring occasionally. Cool. Keep refrigerated. Will keep for 1 week.

To serve, sandwich meringues together with cream and pour curd over.

CUSTOMER FAVOURITES

Every year around Easter time my sister and I share a bottle of wine and reflect upon this thing we created called Lamonts. We were such novices when we opened our restaurant at our parents' winery at Easter in 1989. What we had was a passion for food and a belief that we could do 'it'. What 'it' was we often wonder!

The most wonderful thing about our business is our regular customers, people who supported us when we started out, helped us along the way, not only by spending money with us, but by encouraging us, criticising us in a gentle and constructive way, and praising us when they felt we deserved it: they rewarded us with their return business and by bringing their friends to share meals and wine with us year after year.

Roast capsicum soup

serves 6

In the early days, having alfresco at Lamonts was a fairly primitive experience, especially in winter. Customers would huddle in cellar sales, sampling red wine before coming up to the side window of the restaurant and buying mugs of soup, then searching for a spot to sit, away from the wind. I like to think it was the soup they loved but maybe it was the glass of Navera or Vintage port they had as 'one for the road' that really pleased them!

6 red capsicums
2 onions, sliced
6 ripe tomatoes
3 cloves garlic
50 mls olive oil
1 litre chicken stock
100 mls white wine
2 tablespoons balsamic vinegar
1 tablespoon honey
salt and pepper
400 g red emperor
125 mls cream

Roast capsicums drizzled with olive oil in a moderate oven until the skins start to blacken and blister — about 30 minutes. Place straight into a plastic bag or cover with foil until cool to help steam the skins from the flesh. Peel, reserve flesh and any juice, discard skins. Skin and deseed tomatoes. Sauté onions and garlic until soft over medium heat, turn heat to high and add white wine and vinegar. Reduce by boiling for 2 minutes. Lower heat, add tomatoes, capsicum pieces plus any reserved juice, honey and stock. Simmer for 15 minutes. Puree and season. Cube fish pieces and drop into soup. Cook for 5 minutes. Stir in cream. Distribute fish evenly amongst plates, cover with soup, garnish with snipped chives and serve.

Yellow prawn curry

serves 6

There is a school of thought that says wine and curry don't go. It's got some truth in it for sure, but I must say that the flavours of the aromatic spiced, rather than chilli hot, curry can match with a robust oaky white or a punchy medium-bodied red. Regardless, this curry is much loved and requested at Lamonts.

1 onion
4 cloves garlic
60 mls vegetable oil
1 tablespoon cardamon
2 teaspoons chilli powder
2 teaspoons tumeric
2 tablespoons ground coriander
1 tablespoon paprika
2 teaspoons salt
1 cinnamon quill
1 whole star anise
1 tablespoon coriander seeds
2 green chillis
8 coriander stalks and roots, washed
(reserve leaves for finished curry)
10 cm piece of fresh ginger
1 tablespoon sugar
125 mls fish sauce
125 mls soya bean sauce (not soy sauce)
600 mls coconut milk
36 green king or tiger prawns
(about 1 1/2 kg), cleaned
250 g snow peas

Sauté onion and garlic in oil until translucent. Dry fry the cinnamon, star anise and coriander seeds, grind and reserve. Add all other spices to the onion and cook over low heat for 10 minutes. Add dry-fried spice mix and cook for a further 5 minutes. Add sugar, fish sauce, soya bean sauce and coconut milk. Simmer gently for 15 minutes. Cook prawns in curry, add snow peas just a couple of minutes before serving. Serve with rice and coriander leaves.

Chicken with grapes and tarragon

In summer I sometimes think that we make more of this chicken salad than all the other food put together. This salad is unquestionably a customer favourite.

4 large chicken breasts, skinned
3 bay leaves
400 g seedless grapes
200 g snap peas
100 g snow pea sprouts
6 Lebanese cucumbers
1 bunch English spinach
1 egg
salt and pepper
250 mls medium-bodied olive oil
50 mls tarragon vinegar
1 teaspoon dried tarragon

Poach the breasts in simmering salted water flavoured with bay leaves for about 10 minutes. Cool. Wash the grapes and carefully remove from stalks. Top and tail the snap peas and blanch for a minute or two. Refresh in cold water immediately. Slice the cucumbers diagonally. Trim the ends from the shoots. Wash and dry the spinach. Make a light mayonnaise by mixing the egg with the vinegar, tarragon and seasoning in a food processor. With the motor running, gradually pour oil down the chute. Check taste — it should be balanced in terms of acid and salt. Shred the chicken and mix with all ingredients. Serve.

Chocolate brownie
to fit a 32 cm x 26 cm x 5 cm tin

This brownie is the chicken salad of the cake section at the shop. It's moist, chocolatey and, in my opinion, best served with vanilla icecream — although I suspect most of it is eaten straight from the bag and never makes it home from St Georges Terrace!

275 g butter
330 g light brown soft sugar
2 teaspoons vanilla essence
4 large eggs
550 g chocolate, melted
160 g plain flour
1 teaspoon baking powder
120 g walnuts
1 cup sour cream

Cream butter and sugar with vanilla. Add eggs one at a time, beating each egg in well. Add melted chocolate and mix well. Fold dry ingredients with sour cream. Pour into a greased and lined tray and bake for 40 minutes in a preheated 180°C oven until the brownie is just coming away from the sides of the tin. It will fall and crack on top. Cool in tin and slice when cold.

PERSONAL FAVOURITES

I'm frequently asked what my favourite dishes are and my answer is most often, 'Oh, just about everything!' — and that is fairly accurate, I love to eat! I don't know how you could work in the food industry if you didn't. I can't imagine what it would be like not wanting to taste and try everything!

There is no doubt in my mind that the best cooks love to eat the food they prepare. In many ways all the recipes in this book are personal favourites. I have cooked and eaten all of them many times. In virtually all instances they invoke a fondness of a personal and professional nature, and most of the time I have enjoyed them with wine. Food is to be enjoyed, and is an integral part of the way that I live.

Goats cheese salad
serves 6

This salad has been on our menus for years, for me it is one of the most delicious meals you can eat. It has all the things that make simple fresh food such a powerful force. It has texture and flavour; creamy smooth cheese, crunchy substantial crumbs, crisp yet soft greens and a gentle sweet sharpness from the vinaigrette. Use the best olive oil you can, both in the marinade and the vinaigrette. It is a standard starter if you dine at my home, and one of the few meals I would cook for myself. Guess I can't say enough about it!

3 fresh goats cheese, about 150 g each
6 x 1 cm slices of sourdough or other sturdy bread
250 mls olive oil
$\frac{1}{3}$ cup roughly chopped oregano
$\frac{1}{3}$ cup roughly chopped thyme
$\frac{1}{3}$ cup roughly chopped parsley
$\frac{1}{2}$ teaspoon salt
1 teaspoon cracked black pepper
6 generous cups washed salad leaves
(baby cos, mizzuna, butternut crunch)

Raspberry Vinaigrette Dressing

50 mls raspberry vinegar
150 mls olive oil
salt and pepper

Slice goats cheese in half horizontally. Combine oil, seasoning and herbs and marinate cheese for a minimum of 12 hours — up to a week is fine. Make dressing by combining vinegar, oil and seasoning. Crumble bread into coarse crumbs. Ten minutes prior to serving, dip each cheese into crumbs, retaining some of the herbs and oil on the cheese. Place on oven tray. Drizzle the remaining oil and herbs from the marinade over the crumbed cheeses. Bake in preheated 180°C oven for 5–7 minutes, until cheese is warmed through and the crumbs take on a crunchy feel. Dress salad leaves. Distribute leaves onto plates and serve a cheese on top of each salad.

Chicken and sweet potato risotto
serves 8

Risotto is enjoying high status on restaurant menus these days, and deservedly so, as it can be both elegant and comforting at the same time. Go to the effort of buying the appropriate rice and make some stock. This is one dish that I feel really rewards the maker, and I love it for that (and the fact that it's a one bowl meal!).

500 g Arborio or Carnaroli rice
1200 mls of chicken stock
3 or 4 medium sweet potatoes
500 g chicken breast,
cut into 1 cm cubes
1 medium onion, diced finely
3 cloves garlic, minced
salt and pepper
250 mls white wine
125 g parmesan cheese
$1/2$ cup flatleaf parsley
olive oil

Peel and dice sweet potato into 2 cm pieces. Place on baking tray, drizzle with olive oil, season and roast in moderate oven for about 25 minutes until softened but still holding shape. In a large sized saucepan (big enough to hold all the stock and as much again) sauté onion and garlic in about 2 tablespoons of olive oil over medium heat until translucent. Heat stock in a separate saucepan. Add rice to onion and garlic and turn heat to high. Fry rice for about 2 minutes so that all the grains are coated in oil, taking care to stir constantly as the rice must not colour. Add wine and reduce until most is absorbed. Turn heat down to medium and add a ladle (about 200 mls) of heated stock to rice, stirring gently. Add stock a ladle at a time with a pinch of salt occasionally, and stir constantly and gently. It should take about 15–20 minutes for the stock to be absorbed. When you feel the rice is nearly cooked (it should be just firm to bite at this stage and quite creamy), add in the pieces of chicken, stirring to move the meat through the risotto. The heat will cook the chicken as the rice finishes cooking. When chicken is cooked, fold in sweet potato, check seasoning and fold in parmesan and parsley. Serve immediately.

Lemon polenta cake
for a 28 cm tin

This recipe is based on one in The River Cafe Cook Book, *and has been a personal favourite from the first time I made it. The cake has a quirky character, is moist yet crumbly, has a grittiness that is welcoming not disconcerting, and accompanies sweet white wine with much virtue. Its crust may become a little dark when you bake it, but don't worry because the cake inside is a joy.*

450 g unsalted butter
450 g caster sugar
6 eggs
450 g almond meal
2 teaspoons vanilla essence
juice of 1 lemon
zest of 4 lemons
225 g fine plain polenta
1½ teaspoons baking powder
¼ teaspoon salt

Cream butter and sugar. Add vanilla. Add eggs one at a time, mixing thoroughly. Add lemon juice and zest. Mix the almond meal, polenta, baking powder and salt and fold into mixture. Pour into a prepared tin and bake at 170°C for an hour, until it just leaves the edge of the tin and is firm to touch in the centre. Serve with cream or icecream.

KATE LAMONT

Kate Lamont lived in the Swan Valley just outside Perth for the first thirty years of her life. Both her parents have long family associations with the Swan Valley, in winemaking and agriculture. In the seventies, Kate's parents, Neil and Corin, began making wine for their own consumption, before commencing commercial production in the early eighties.

Kate discovered a passion for cooking while pursuing a career as a winemaker. Deliberately seeking the broadest possible range of experience, she worked as everything from kitchen hand to short-order cook. Then, in the mid eighties, with the support of their parents, Kate and her sister Fiona opened the restaurant at Lamont's winery.

With the emphasis on fresh, simple, regional food, the restaurant has proved a great and enduring success. It has received many accolades, is a regular finalist in the highly regarded American Express Best Restaurant Awards and, in 1998, was awarded Best Winery Restaurant in the inaugural RCA awards.

In the mid nineties, seeking to expand the business, Kate and Fiona opened a Lamonts outlet in St Georges Terrace, Perth. The focus of the shop is on fine produce, catering, take out and hampers. This city presence has put Lamonts in the forefront of Perth's food scene. Kate's latest venture is the opening of a new restaurant in East Perth.

As a partner of the Lamont's family businesses, in 1996 Kate was honoured with the Telstra Businesswoman of the Year Award, in the business owner category. Despite her obvious corporate nous, however, Kate prefers the kitchen to the boardroom. Her first loves are cooking and hospitality, and they are at the very heart of her success.

INDEX

• A •

anchovies	14
asparagus with roasted garlic dressing	62

• B •

balsamic vinegar	14
barbequed squid	50
brownie, chocolate	83

• C •

cake	
lemon polenta	91
orange almond	59
capers	14
capsicum soup	78
caramel slice	46
caramelised onions	20
chicken	
and spinach salad with mustard dressing	34
and sweet potato risotto	88
rissoles with lemon oil	42

chicken *contd*.
    stock 29
    with grapes and tarragon 82
chilli mayonnaise 51
chocolate brownie 83
coriander sauce 54
corn, spinach and goats cheese linguine 32
cos lettuce salad 66
couscous with roasted pumpkin and cashews 55
curry, yellow prawn 81

• D •

dressing
    see also sauce
    mustard 34
    olive oil and vinegar 56, 86
    raspberry vinaigrette 86
    roasted garlic 62
    simple salad 56, 66, 86
    sweet Thai-style 70
    tarragon mayonnaise 82

• F •

fish
    salmon with sweet Thai-style dressing 70
    sauce 14
    stock 28
    tandoori fish salad 64

• G •

garlic dressing	62
goats cheese	
salad	86
spinach and corn linguine	32
greens with blue cheese croutons and field mushroom slices	56
grilled	
chicken and spinach salad	34
quail	52
salmon with sweet Thai-style dressing	70

• L •

lamb	
fillets with coriander sauce	54
with yoghurt in flatbread	45
lemon	
oil	14
polenta cake	91
preserved	22
linguine with goats cheese, spinach and corn	32

• M •

mascapone cream with strawberries	67
mayonnaise	
chilli	51
tarragon	82

meringues with passionfruit curd	74
mushroom soup with crispy bacon pieces	35
mustard dressing	34

• O •

olive oil	14, 15
olive oil and vinegar dressing	56, 86
olive tapenade	44
onions, caramelised	20
orange almond cake	59

• P •

passionfruit curd	74
pasta	17
pepper	16
porcini mushrooms with veal steaks	72
potato slice with tapenade	43
prawn curry	81
preserved lemons	22
puff pastry	24
puff pastry tarts	41

• Q •

quail, grilled	52
quick puff pastry tarts	41
quick rough puff pastry	24

• R •

red wine vinegar	14
rhubarb and raspberry roly-poly	36
risotto, chicken and sweet potato	88
rissoles, chicken with lemon oil	42
roast capsicum soup	78
roasted	
garlic dressing	62
tomatoes	21
vegetables	73
roly-poly, rhubarb and raspberry	36

• S •

salad	
chicken and spinach	34
chicken with grapes and tarragon	82
cos lettuce	66
goats cheese	86
greens with blue cheese croutons and field mushroom slices	56
tandoori fish	64
salmon, grilled with sweet Thai-style dressing	70
salsa verde	23
salt	14, 16
sauce	
see also dressing	
coriander	54
fish	14
salsa verde	23
seasoning	16

soup
    mushroom with crispy bacon pieces 35
    roast capsicum 78
spicy lamb with yoghurt in flatbread 45
spinach
    goats cheese and corn linguine 32
    grilled chicken and mustard dressing 34
squid, barbequed 50
stock 26
    chicken 29
    fish 28
strawberries with mascapone cream 67

• T •

tandoori fish salad 64
tandoori paste 64
tapenade 44
tarragon mayonnaise 82
tarts 41
Thai-style dressing 70
tomatoes, roasted 21

• V •

veal steaks with porcini mushrooms 72
vegetables, roasted 73
vinegar 14
vinegar and olive oil dressing 56, 86

• W •

wine and food   11

• Y •

yellow prawn curry   81

First published 2000 by
FREMANTLE ARTS CENTRE PRESS
PO Box 158, North Fremantle
Western Australia 6159.
http://www.facp.iinet.net.au

Copyright text © Kate Lamont, 2000.
Copyright photographs © Greg Hocking, 2000.

This book is copyright. Apart from any fair dealing for the purpose of
private study, research, criticism or review, as permitted under the
Copyright Act, no part may be reproduced by any process without written permission.
Enquiries should be made to the publisher.

Consulting Editor Cate Sutherland.
Designer Marion Duke.

Typeset by Fremantle Arts Centre Press
and printed by Sands Print Group, Bassendean, Western Australia.

National Library of Australia
Cataloguing-in-publication data

Lamont, Kate, 1962—.
Family, food and friends.

ISBN 1 86368 293 7.

I. Lamont, Kate, 1962 - Anecdotes. 2. Cookery. I. Title.

641

The State of Western Australia has made an investment in this project
through ArtsWA in association with the Lotteries Commission.